Raw Food Cookbook

Simple, Quick, Natural and
Tasty Meals for Your
Healthy Raw Food Lifestyle

Printed in the United States of America.
First Printing, 2013

Table of Contents

Josephine James

Introduction

Eating raw foods is not just a passing trend, many people are seeing the health benefits of consuming raw foods. Whether you follow a 100% raw diet or you are just looking to consume more raw foods to improve your eating habits, then this recipe collection can help to add variety to your meal plan.

All of the recipes in this book use only 100% raw ingredients. It is important be aware of a few ingredients when you are doing your grocery shopping, so you can be sure you are buying truly raw ingredients.

These are a few ingredients to watch out for:

Spices: Many of the recipes include the use of spices, but not all spices are created equal... it depends on the type of spices you are using. Some strict raw foodists claim that spices aren't raw because they may have been heated to high temperatures. Certain spices can be harvested and preserved raw, because they use a low temperature drying method that doesn't heat the leaves.

It is possible to buy raw spices online or at health food stores, you just need to read the labels to understand what you are getting.

Honey or Agave: Both of these sweeteners can be purchased raw or conventional (heated). Again, it is important to read the labels and understand the source in order to determine if the product is truly raw.

Salt: Certain types of salt can be used on a raw food diet, because it is possible to harvest the salt without heating the product. For example, sea salt can be collected by allowing the salt water to evaporate, which leaves the salt behind. Just be sure you are buying a quality brand that specifically states that it is raw.

Vanilla: Grocery stores carry "vanilla extract" which is definitely not raw... and there isn't much real vanilla in the bottle. Any recipe that calls for vanilla is referring to pure vanilla, which can be made using whole vanilla beans or purchased online or at the health food store.

Cacao: Chocolate coco powder at the grocery store has been heated and highly processed, so it is not a raw ingredient. Instead of using conventional chocolate powder, look for raw cacao which is delicious to use in many dessert recipes.

Apple Cider Vinegar: Most brands of apple cider vinegar are not raw, and the processing has removed the beneficial enzymes and health benefits from the vinegar. Look for a vinegar that is specifically labeled as "raw," such as the Bragg's brand.

Nama Shoyu: This ingredient is a great way to add flavor to many raw dishes, although it's important to buy Nama Shoyu that is specifically labeled as "raw." It is a type of unpasteurized soy sauce that contains living enzymes.

Raw Nuts: Many of the recipes use nuts, and you should always buy raw nuts instead of roasted or blanched nuts. Most nuts at the grocery store have been cooked, so you need to verify the source and read the packaging to make sure the nuts haven't been heated. Some of the recipes call for soaked nuts, which means that the nuts should be submersed in water to activate the enzymes. If the recipe calls for soaked nuts, they should be soaked for 8 hours and drained, unless otherwise noted.

As you begin preparing raw food recipes, you will see that there are certain kitchen tools that are necessary to make some of the recipes. For example, many of the recipes use a food processor, which allows you to chop and slice ingredients quickly and easily. A food processor is nice because it saves time when you are in the kitchen, and allows you to create recipes that aren't possible to make by hand.

Another tool that you will want to have is a high speed blender, such as a VitaMix or a BlendTec. Standard, cheap blenders won't be sufficient to get the right, smooth texture that is needed for many of the ingredients. A high speed blender is pricey, but worth it because it is much more effective than using a cheap blender.

Dehydrators are popular kitchen tools among raw food enthusiasts, because they are a great way to prepare foods with different textures and tastes. It is best that you purchase a high quality dehydrator that gives you temperature control. Some of the cheaper dehydrators don't allow you to manage the temperature, which means the foods could be dried at a higher temperature which will kill the living enzymes within the food.

With a little practice, you will see that these recipes will expand your menu and allow you to easily include more healthy foods into your daily habits. These recipes are easy to make, delicious, and full of nutrition.

Josephine James

Raw Breakfast Recipes

It has been said that breakfast is the most important meal of the day. Just because you are eating raw foods doesn't mean that you should miss out on popular breakfast dishes. These recipes are good replacements for common cooked breakfasts, and they are packed with nutrition to help get your day started right.

The great thing about raw foods is that some of the recipes use a dehydrator, so you can make the recipe the night before and let it dry while you are sleeping. In the morning, you will have a warm breakfast ready when you wake up.

Instead of eating boring, plain fruit every morning, use these recipes to add a little variety to your breakfast menu. The recipes are filling, to give you the energy that you need to make it through the day.

Banana Oat Pancakes

Ingredients:

2 cups oat groats, soaked for at least 8 hours

6 bananas, peeled

1 cup ground flax seed

Directions:

After soaking the oat groats for at least 8 hours, rinse well and drain excess water.

In a food processor, combine the banana and goats. Process well, until the mixture has a batter consistency. Stir in the ground flax by hand.

Place the batter onto teflex dehydrator sheets, forming rounds with about a quarter cup of batter in each pancake. Dehydrate overnight.

In the morning, top with fresh fruit and raw maple syrup.

Cherry Granola

Ingredients:

2 apples, seeds and stem removed, chopped

2 cups almonds, soaked

2 cups buckwheat, rinsed & soaked

3 cups pecans, soaked

1/2 cup walnuts, soaked

1 cup pumpkin seeds

1 cup cherries, dried

1 cup dates, soaked, save some of the soak water

1 cup flax seeds

1/2 cup fresh orange juice

1/2 cup maple syrup

1 tablespoon vanilla

1 tablespoon orange zest

2 teaspoons cinnamon

2 teaspoons sea salt

Directions:

In the food processor, add the dates, orange juice, orange zest, maple syrup, salt, walnuts, cinnamon, 1 apple, and about 1/4 cup of the water from the soaked dates. Run in the food processor until smooth and well incorporated. Transfer mixture into a larger mixing bowl.

After the food processor has been emptied, add the 2nd apple, pecans, and almonds. Pulse the food processor a few times to chop everything. Add the apple and nut mixture to the smooth mixture in the mixing bowl.

Add the rest of the ingredients into the mixing bowl, and stir by hand. Spread evenly on teflex dehydrator trays. Dehydrate for 8 hours at 115 degrees, then move granola from the teflex sheets to mesh dehydrator trays. Continue dehydrating until it is crunchy enough, usually another 6 hours.

Remove from the dehydrator, break into chunks. Cool completely before storing.

Chia Pudding

Ingredients:

1 cup almond milk

4 tablespoons chia seed

1/2 - 1 cup chopped fruit

cinnamon to taste

vanilla powder to taste

Directions:

Pour the almond milk and chia seed into a bowl, let it sit for 15 minutes or until the chia has soaked up the milk. Stir in the chopped fruit. Cinnamon and vanilla are optional to sweeten and add taste.

Strawberry Chia Pudding

Ingredients:

1 cup almond milk

1/3 cup dried chia seeds

7 - 8 strawberries

2 teaspoons pure vanilla

Directions:

In the blender, combine the almond milk, strawberries, and vanilla. Blend well to a smooth consistency.

Put the chia seeds in a bowl, and pour the strawberry mixture over the top and stir together. Let it sit for 3 or 4 minutes, then stir well. Allow it to sit for another 20 minutes, stir well and serve.

Oat Groats

Ingredients:

1/4 cup oat groats

2 apples, chopped and separated

1/4 cup water

1 teaspoon cinnamon

1 tablespoon agave

1/4 cup raisins

small handful of walnuts

Directions:

Soak the oat groats overnight, rinse well in the morning and drain excess water. In the blender, add the oat groats, 1 apple, water, cinnamon, and agave. Blend well.

In a small bowl, add the 2nd chopped apple, raisins, walnuts, and pour the blender mixture over the top.

Breakfast Bars

Ingredients:

3 apples, shredded

3 apples, chopped

1 cup ground almonds

3/4 cup ground walnuts

1/2 cup ground flax seeds

1 cup honey

1-1/2 cup dried currants, soaked

1 teaspoon apple pie spice

Directions:

Stir everything together in a large mixing bowl. Form the mixture into patties, and lay on dehydrator trays. Dehydrate at 105 degrees for 24 hours.

Banana Crepes

Ingredients:

4 bananas, peeled

1 lemon, juiced

1 cup cashews, soaked

2 young coconuts, pulp only (water removed)

1 tablespoon agave

1 teaspoon vanilla

Fresh berries

Directions:

Make the banana crepes by adding the bananas and lemon juice to the blender. Blend until smooth.

Pour the banana mixture onto teflex dehydrator sheets, in circles about 5 inches in diameter. Dehydrate at 100 degrees overnight, about 8 hours. Don't dehydrate too long, because you want them to still be flexible.

In the morning, make the cream by combining the cashews, coconut pulp, agave, and vanilla in the blender. Blend until smooth.

Assemble the crepes by spreading with a little bit of cashew cream, topping with berries, and folding the crepe. Top with another spoonful of cashew cream if desired.

Breakfast Quiche

Crust Ingredients:

1 1/2 cup soaked pecans

1 tablespoon water to combine

1 tablespoon psyllium Husk

1 tablespoon Braggs Aminos

1 teaspoon sea salt

Filling Ingredients:

1 cup cashews, soaked

16 ounces baby spinach

1 red bell pepper, chopped

2 leeks, chopped

1 handful dill

1 handful parsley

2 tablespoons fresh lemon Juice

3 tablespoons psyllium husk

1 teaspoon nutmeg

1 tablespoon nutritional yeast

salt and pepper

Directions:

Make the crust by combining all crust ingredients in
the food processor, and process until it is a crumbly
texture. Use a spoon to press the mixture into the
bottom of a pan.

Add all of the filling ingredients to the food processor,
and process until it is a smooth texture. Pour the
mixture over the top of the crust, chill in the fridge for
at least 1 hour before serving.

Raw Bagels

Ingredients:

1 cup almonds, soaked

1 cup cucumber or zucchini

1/2 cup flaxseed

1/4 cup red bell pepper

1/4 cup onion

1/4 teaspoon sea salt

Directions:

In a food processor, add all ingredients and process until smooth. Mold the dough into 4 bagel shaped mounds on teflex dehydrator sheets.

Dehydrate 6 hours 100 degrees, then turn the bagels over onto mesh dehydrator trays. Continue dehydrating another 2 - 4 hours. You want them to dry but not be crispy, they should still be a little flexible.

Sprouted Oatmeal

Ingredients:

3/4 cup hull-less oats (oats that are sproutable)

1/4 cup almond milk

1/4 cup walnuts

1/4 cup raisins, divided

2 tablespoons sunflower seeds

1 tablespoon maple syrup

1/2 teaspoon vanilla

Optional: cinnamon, berries, shredded coconut, bananas, etc.

Directions:

Soak the oats and nuts overnight. Rinse and drain them in the morning.

Add the oats, nuts, almond milk, 1/2 of the raisins, maple syrup, and vanilla in a food processor. Pulse until a good, chewy texture is achieved. Add more milk if needed.

Place the oatmeal in a bowl, garnish with more nuts, cinnamon, chopped fruit, or any other ingredients that you would like to use.

Raw Main Meal Recipes

Dinner time is the perfect time to share a good meal with family and friends, and there are many satisfying raw recipes to share with your family. Many people have a hard time understanding how it is possible to be full and satisfied after eating only raw foods, but these recipes are designed to be very satisfying. You will be able to enjoy the meal, knowing that the meal is packed with good enzymes and nutrients that are available in raw foods.

These main meal recipes can be used for lunch or dinner. Often, I like to make extra and keep it in the fridge for the next day. Many of the recipes have been created to mimic popular cooked dishes, so you can enjoy a healthier version of your favorite comfort foods.

Mango Spring Rolls

Ingredients:

1 cup red cabbage, thinly sliced

1 1/4 cup Napa cabbage, thinly sliced

1/4 cup carrots, peeled and julienned

2/3 cup green onions, julienned

2/3 cup red bell pepper, julienned

2/3 cup radish, julienned

1/2 cup cilantro leaves, stems removed

1/3 cup raw almonds, chopped

Mint leaves

Wraps: either lettuce leaves or seaweed sheets

Mango Sauce Ingredients:

3/4 cup mango, chopped

6 dates, pitted and soaked for 2 hours

1/4 cup fresh orange juice

1/4 cup fresh lemon juice

1 garlic clove

1/4 cup onion, chopped

1 1/2 tablespoon nama shoyu

1/4 teaspoon jalapeno, minced

1/2 teaspoon fresh ginger, minced

Directions:

Make the mango sauce first, combining the dates, onion, mango, citrus juice, jalapeno, ginger, garlic, and nama shoyu in a blender. Blend well, until smooth. Store in the refrigerator.

Assemble the spring rolls by filling the lettuce wraps with the cabbage, bell pepper, radish, carrots, and green onions. The recipe makes about 8 wraps, so divide the stuffing ingredients evenly. Arrange the vegetables in the lettuce wrap, sprinkle chopped almonds on top and add a mint leaf and a few cilantro leaves. Roll up the lettuce leaf, and serve immediately.

Serve the lettuce wraps with the mango sauce on the side. Or, the mango sauce can be drizzled inside the wraps.

Josephine James

Raw Thai Curry

Ingredients:

1/4 cup red bell pepper, diced

1/4 cup sweet potato, diced

1/4 cup broccoli, grated

1/4 cup cauliflower, grated

1/4 cup carrot, grated

1 tablespoon currants, soaked for 30 minutes

1 cup greens, chopped (kale or spinach is usually best)

Curry Sauce Ingredients:

2 cups fresh coconut, water and meat

1/4 cup almond milk

2 teaspoons fresh lime juice

1 parsnip, juiced

2 teaspoon fresh ginger juice

1/2 teaspoon coriander, ground

1 teaspoon lemongrass

1/2 cup fresh cilantro

Directions:

In a blender, combine all curry sauce ingredients and blend well to a smooth consistency.

Add all other ingredients to a large bowl, pour the curry sauce on top. Garnish with fresh cilantro leaves for decoration.

Raw Garden Burgers

Ingredients:

1 pound carrots, shredded

1 pound sunflower seeds, ground

1 red bell pepper, minced

1 sweet onion, minced

3 tablespoons nutritional yeast

2 tablespoons Mrs. Dash seasoning blend

1 teaspoon sage, fresh

1 tablespoon basil, fresh

1 tablespoon raw honey

1 tablespoon extra virgin olive oil

1 teaspoon sea salt

Directions:

In a large mixing bowl, combine all ingredients and
mix well.

Use your hands to form the mixture into burger patties.
Serve on top of fresh lettuce leaves, and include
condiments such as raw barbeque sauce, sliced
tomatoes, sliced onion, raw pickles, etc.

Raw Fajitas

Ingredients:

1 red bell pepper, thinly sliced

1/4 onion, thinly sliced

10 mushrooms, thinly sliced

1 carrot, grated

1/2 zucchini, thinly sliced

Lettuce leaves for wraps

1/3 cup walnuts, chopped

Fajita Sauce Ingredients:

1 garlic clove, minced

1 tablespoon extra virgin olive oil

1/2 teaspoon sea salt

1 tablespoon agave

1/2 tablespoon fresh lime juice

1/4 teaspoon cumin

1/4 teaspoon cayenne pepper

1 teaspoon paprika

Directions:

In a mixing bowl, add all sauce ingredients and stir
well to incorporate. Add the sliced vegetables, and coat
with the sauce. Try to submerge all the vegetables in
the sauce, marinate in the fridge for at least 4 hours.

Fill lettuce leaves with marinated fajita stuffing and
serve immediately.

Josephine James

Rice Bowl

Ingredients:

1 head cauliflower, grated

2 lemons, juiced

2 garlic cloves

1 tablespoon raw sesame seeds

1/2 teaspoon ginger, grated

6 tablespoons nama shoyu

4 tablespoons raw honey

1/4 teaspoon sea salt

3 cups of chopped vegetables, such as cabbage, carrots, bell peppers, broccoli, mushrooms, etc.

Directions:

In a blender, add the lemon juice, garlic, sesame seeds, ginger, nama shoyu, honey, and sea salt. Blend well.

Use the grated cauliflower as the rice base in the bottom of the bowl, add chopped vegetables on top. Pour the sauce over everything and enjoy.

Spanish Cauliflower Rice

Ingredients:

1 head cauliflower, grated

1 mashed avocado

1 orange bell pepper, diced

2 tomatoes, diced

4 green onions, diced

1 jalapeno, seeded & diced (keep the seeds if you want it spicy)

1/4 cup cilantro, chopped

2 tablespoons fresh lemon juice

1/4 cup extra virgin olive oil

1 teaspoon paprika

1 teaspoon chili powder

1 teaspoon sea salt

Directions:

Combine all of the ingredients in a large mixing bowl,
stir well to evenly coat the vegetables in the
seasonings, avocado and oil.

Zucchini Pesto

Ingredients:

1 tablespoon garlic, minced

1/3 cup walnuts

1/3 cup pine nuts

1/2 cup extra virgin olive oil

1 1/2 cups fresh basil

1 lemon, juiced

Zucchini, spiraled to make spaghetti noodles

Diced tomatoes for garnishment

Directions:

Add all ingredients except zucchini and tomatoes into a blender or food processor. Blend until a good, creamy consistency is achieved.

Pour sauce over the zucchini noodles, garnish with diced tomatoes, serve immediately.

Pizza Crust

Ingredients:

4 cups zucchini, peel removed and chopped

4 cups buckwheat, soaked

2 1/2 cups sunflower seeds, soaked

1 cup flax seed, ground

1/4 cup extra virgin olive oil

1 1/4 cups water

1 tablespoon crushed garlic

3 tablespoon Italian herbs

1 teaspoon sea salt

Directions:

In a food processor, combine all ingredients and blend until good, smooth consistency is achieved. Spread on teflex dehydrator sheets, about 1/4 inch thick.
Dehydrate at 110 degrees for 2 hours, cut into pieces and then flip.
Continue dehydrating 6 - 8 hours until desired texture is reached. Don't over dry, you want the texture to still be chewy (not too crispy).

Top with any pizza toppings, such as diced tomatoes, chopped basil, onion, etc.

Eggplant Pizza

Ingredients:

2 medium eggplants, thinly sliced

1 cup pine nuts

1 pitted date, soaked

1 clove garlic

1 cup spinach

1 cup sun dried tomatoes, soaked

1/2 cup mushrooms, finely chopped

Josephine James

Directions:

Soak the sundried tomatoes for at least 4 hours, drain well.

In a food processor, add the pine nuts and date, process until smooth. Add in the spinach, garlic and sundried tomatoes, pulse to incorporate all ingredients.

Use the eggplant slices as the pizza crust, smooth tomato mixture over the top and sprinkle the mushrooms on top. Dehydrate at 115 degrees until desired crispiness is achieved.

Alfredo Mushroom Linguine

Ingredients:

2 yellow squash, spiraled

2 1/2 cups sliced mushrooms

2 garlic cloves

2 tablespoons Nama Shoyu

3 tablespoons olive oil

2 teaspoons apple cider vinegar

1 teaspoons raw honey

1/4 cup parsley, chopped

Alfredo Sauce Ingredients:

1 1/2 cups cashews, soaked

1/3 cup fresh lemon juice

2 garlic cloves, minced

1/2 cup pine nuts

6 tablespoons olive oil

1 teaspoon nutritional yeast

2/3 cup water

1 tsp sea salt

Directions:

Spiral the squash noodles, or use a vegetable peeler to create thin squash noodles. Set aside.

Marinate the mushrooms in the olive oil, nama shoyu, apple cider vinegar, garlic and honey. Let the mixture sit for 30 minutes, then drain.

Make the Alfredo sauce in a blender. Add in all sauce ingredients and blend until it is a smooth, creamy consistency.

Put the noodles on a plate, top with the marinated mushrooms, and pour the sauce over the top. Use the parsley to garnish the plate.

Corn and Avocado Boats

Ingredients:

1 avocado

1 cup corn

1/4 red onion, chopped

1/4 red bell pepper, chopped

1/4 tomato, chopped

pinch of red pepper

pinch of sea salt

Directions:

Slice the avocados in half, scoop out the avocado flesh and discard the pits. Mash the avocado in a bowl, stir in the corn, onion, bell pepper, red pepper and sea salt.

Fill the avocado shells with the mixture, top with tomatoes for garnishment.

Mushroom Loaf

Ingredients:

2 1/2 portabella mushrooms

1/2 cup sun dried tomatoes

1/2 cup carrots

1 cup walnuts

1/2 red bell pepper

1 tablespoon parsley, chopped

1 garlic clove

1 inch poblano pepper piece

1 teaspoon sea salt

1/2 teaspoon cumin

Directions:

Add everything into a food processor, process to form an even consistency. Shape into a loaf, top with raw barbeque sauce.
Dehydrate at 100 degrees for 10 - 12 hours, best when served warm.

Cheezy Broccoli

Ingredients:

3 cups broccoli, finely chopped

1 teaspoon Braggs Liquid Aminos

1 tablespoon melted coconut oil

2 tablespoons raw tahini

2 tablespoons hemp seeds

1 tablespoon nutritional yeast

1 1/2 teaspoon lemon juice

1/4 teaspoon paprika

1/8 teaspoon garlic powder

Directions:

In a small mixing bowl, combine all ingredients except broccoli. Whisk well to incorporate all ingredients. Pour sauce over broccoli, toss to coat evenly, and serve immediately.

Josephine James

Mushroom Burger

Ingredients:

2 cups walnuts

1 red onion, chopped

3 carrots, chopped

1/4 cup dates

2 tablespoons olive oil

1 teaspoon honey

1 teaspoon balsamic vinegar

1 teaspoon sea salt

1/4 bunch dill, fresh

Portobello mushrooms

Directions:

Add everything except the mushrooms to the food processor, process until a good consistency is achieved. Form the mixture into burger patties, use a Portobello mushroom as the "bun." Top with raw condiments of your choice, avocado, barbeque sauce, mayo, pickles, lettuce.

Alternatively, if you don't want that much mushroom, try substituting the mushroom for lettuce leaves and make a wrap instead.

Zucchini and Bell Pepper Patties

Ingredients:

3 zucchinis, shredded and divided

1 red bell pepper, chopped

1-1/2 C walnuts, soaked

1 cup flax, ground

1/4 cup scallions

1 tablespoon red pepper flakes

Directions:

Set aside 1/3 of the shredded zucchini. Add the rest of the zucchini, bell pepper, flax, walnuts, and red pepper flakes into the food processor. Pulse a few times to grind everything together and get a good consistency.

In a large mixing bowl, combine the rest of the zucchini with the mixture from the food processor. Stir in the scallions, and mix well by hand.

Form the mixture into patties, dehydrate on teflex sheets at 115 degrees for 6 hours. Flip the patties and place them on mesh dehydrator sheets, continue dehydrating for another 6 hours.

The goal is to have a crispy texture on the outside of the patties, and a soft texture on the inside.

Top with any condiments that you prefer, such as raw ranch dip or barbeque sauce.

Josephine James

Cheezy Zucchini Bites

Ingredients:

1 zucchini, sliced

1 tablespoon extra virgin olive oil

1 tablespoon almonds, ground

2 teaspoons nutritional yeast

Pinch of cayenne pepper

Pinch of sea salt

Pinch of black pepper

Directions:

In a mixing bowl, add everything except the zucchini. Stir well to combine the ingredients.

Add the zucchini, and evenly coat the zucchini pieces. It is easiest to use your hands to massage the seasonings into the zucchini.

Indian Cauliflower Korma

Ingredients:

1/2 cup onion, chopped

1/2 cup Carrot, chopped

1 red bell pepper, chopped

1/2 cup cashews

1 garlic clove

1 tomato, chopped

2 tablespoons curry powder (mild is best if you don't want too much spice)

2 tablespoons Water

2 dates

1 teaspoon chilli powder

Pinch of cumin

Pinch of turmeric

1/4 cup raisins

1/2 head Cauliflower, shredded

Directions:

Set the cauliflower and raisins aside, add the rest of the ingredients into a food processor. Pulse a few times to process everything together. If needed, add more water. The consistency should be thick, but still runny.

Use the food processor to shred the cauliflower, it should be chopped into the texture of trice.

In a large mixing bowl, combine the cauliflower and raisins. Pour the curry sauce over the top, and stir to coat evenly.

Green Bean Casserole

Ingredients:

2 cups green beans

1 cup mushrooms, sliced

1 cup water

1 1/2 tablespoons almond butter

1 tablespoon agave

1 onion, chopped and marinated in Bragg's Liquid Aminos

Directions:

Prepare the onions by marinating them in the Bragg's Liquid Aminos for 3 hours, then dehydrate at 105 degrees for at least 8 hours.

In a blender or food processor, add the agave, mushrooms, almond butter and water. Blend to incorporate all ingredients. In a large mixing bowl add the onions and green beans. Pour the mushroom sauce over the top, stir to evenly coat.

Put into a casserole dish, dehydrate at 105 degrees for 2 hours.

Stuffed Bell Peppers

Ingredients:

2 bell peppers, halved and seeded

2 cups jicama, chopped

2 garlic cloves

1 small avocado, separated

1/4 cup cilantro

1/4 cup corn

1/4 cup olives

1/2 lemon, juiced

1/4 teaspoon chili powder

Pinch of sea salt

Directions:

In a food processor, add the jicima, garlic, cilantro, half of the avocado, lemon, chili powder and salt. Process until combined, maintaining a little bit of a texture (don't over-process).

Stir in the olives and corn by hand. Scoop the filling into the bell pepper halves. Slice the other half of the avocado and garnish the peppers with avocado slices and a few cilantro sprigs.

Josephine James

Raw Salad Recipes

Salads are a great way to enjoy healthy vegetables in beautiful, tasty combinations. It can be easy to get stuck in a rut when making a salad, and get bored of the same toppings and dressing on your salad.

Instead of making the same salad over and over again, these recipes will give you options to add variety to your meals. using raw ingredients you can create dressings and other delicious combinations that will delight your taste buds and leave you feeling satisfied.

Marinated Cucumber Salad

Ingredients:

1 English cucumbers

1 medium red onion

1 tablespoon extra virgin olive oil

3 lemons, juiced

1/2 teaspoon garlic, minced

1 teaspoon Chinese five spice powder

1 1/2 teaspoon sea salt

Raw agave, to taste

Josephine James

Directions:

Thinly slice the cucumbers and onion, add them to a medium size bowl.

In another bowl, mix all other ingredients and whisk together well. Pour the dressing over the onions and cucumbers, stir well to evenly coat. Arrange the cucumbers and onions so they are submerged in the dressing.

Cover the bowl, and store in the fridge for several hours, stirring occasionally. Store in the fridge overnight, serve chilled.

Apple Spinach Salad

Salad Ingredients:

2 handfuls of baby spinach

1 banana, chopped

1 small apple, chopped

1/4 cup raisins

Dressing Ingredients:

3/4 cup water

1/4 cup sunflower seeds

1 teaspoon vanilla

1 teaspoon cinnamon

1 teaspoon agave

pinch of salt

Directions:

Make the dressing by adding all dressing ingredients into the blender, and blend until smooth.

Add the salad ingredients into a medium sized bowl, and pour the dressing over the salad. Stir to coat evenly.

Pea and Broccoli Salad

Ingredients:

1 cup broccoli, chopped into small pieces

1 cup peas

8 grape tomatoes, sliced in half

1 tablespoon honey

1 tablespoon water

1 tablespoon extra virgin olive oil

1 tablespoon grainy raw mustard

Directions:

Combine the honey, water, mustard, and olive oil. Mix well to make the dressing.

Add the broccoli and peas in a mixing bowl, pour the dressing over the top and stir to evenly coat the vegetables.

Other veggie substitutions can be made. Try adding asparagus or cucumber.

Josephine James

Marinated Broccoli Salad

Ingredients:

4 cups broccoli, chopped into bite-size pieces

1/4 cup red or orange bell pepper, chopped

1/3 cup basil, fresh

1/3 cup oregano, fresh

1/4 cup lemon juice, fresh

1/2 cup extra virgin olive oil

1 garlic clove, minced

Directions:

Whisk together the basil, oregano, lemon juice, olive oil, and garlic.

In a mixing bowl, combine the broccoli and red bell pepper. Pour the dressing over the top, stir to evenly coat. Marinate in the fridge for at least 10 hours or more.

Carrot and Apple Salad

Ingredients:

5 large carrots, shredded

2 apples, cored and shredded

1/4 cup dried cranberries

1/4 cup almonds, chopped or slivered

1 lemon, juiced

3 tablespoons honey

Directions:

Add lemon and honey in a bowl, stir well. Add the rest of the ingredients, and coat everything evenly in the dressing.

Cover the bowl, and store in the fridge for at least 8 hours before serving.

Cilantro Cole Slaw

Ingredients:

1/2 head of a small cabbage, shredded

1 scallion, chopped

4 carrots, shredded

1/2 cup cilantro, chopped

1 lemon, juiced

2 garlic cloves, minced

3 tablespoons extra virgin olive oil

2 teaspoons oregano

2 teaspoons cumin

1/2 teaspoon sea salt

Directions:

In a large bowl, add the lemon, garlic, olive oil, oregano, cumin, and salt. Mix well. Add the rest of the ingredients, and stir to coat evenly in the dressing.

"Potato" Salad

Ingredients:

1 cup jicama, diced

1/2 red bell pepper, thinly sliced

1 celery rib, thinly sliced

5 olives, chopped

2 tablespoons chives, chopped

2 teaspoons raw mustard

2 tablespoons raw mayo

Pinch of sea salt

Pinch of freshly ground pepper

Directions:

Combine mayo, mustard, salt, and pepper in a mixing bowl, stir well. Add all other ingredients, stir well to evenly coat with the dressing.

Cucumber Quinoa Salad

Ingredients:

3 cups quinoa, sprouted and rinsed

1 cucumber, diced

1 red bell pepper, diced

1/2 red onion, diced

1/4 cup cashews, chopped

8 - 10 grape tomatoes, sliced in half

1/4 cup extra virgin olive oil

1 lemon, juiced

1 lime, juiced

1 tablespoon tamari

2 garlic cloves, minced

handful of fresh mint, chopped

Leafy greens of your choice

Directions:

Add the tamari, lemon, lime, garlic, and olive oil in a bowl, mix together well. Add the sprouted lentils to the sauce, coat well, and marinate for at least 30 minutes.

Add everything else except the lettuce, toss together to coat the rest of the vegetables with dressing. Serve on a bed of lettuce or any other type of leafy greens.

Apple and Cabbage Salad

Salad Ingredients:

2 cups green cabbage, shredded

2 cups red cabbage, shredded

2 cups apple, sliced thin

1/4 cup sunflower seeds

1/4 cup raisins, soaked

2 teaspoons lemon juice

Dressing Ingredients:

1/4 cup extra virgin olive oil

1 inch ginger, grated

1 lemon, juiced

2 tablespoons tahini

2 teaspoons Nama Shoyu

Directions:

Slice apple, and coat in 2 teaspoons of lemon juice to
prevent browning.

In a mixing bowl, combine all dressing ingredients and
whisk together. Add the salad ingredients, and toss to
evenly coat with dressing. Serve immediately.

Josephine James

Clementine and Fennel Salad

Ingredients:

1 head radicchio

1 head green leaf lettuce

2 heads endive

2 fennel bulbs, sliced

6 Clementines, peeled and segmented

1/2 red onion, thinly sliced

1/4 cup almond slivers

Dressing Ingredients:

1/4 cup extra virgin olive oil

2 garlic cloves, finely minced

3 tablespoons grapefruit juice

2 tablespoons orange juice

1/2 teaspoon orange zest

2 teaspoons ginger root, finely grated

1 teaspoons raw honey

Directions:

Wash all of the leafy vegetables, and tear or chop into salad size pieces. top with the fennel slices, onion, oranges, and almonds.

In a small mixing bowl, whisk together all of the dressing ingredients. Drizzle the dressing on top of the salad and serve immediately.

Waldorf Salad

Ingredients:

1 head Romaine lettuce, chopped

4 apples, diced

3 celery stalks, chopped

1/4 cup red onion, thinly sliced

1 cup red seedless grapes, sliced in half

1/2 cup walnuts, soaked

1/2 cup raisins

1 cup Almond Mayonnaise

Directions:

Add all ingredients in a large mixing bowl and toss together to evenly coat the dressing on the salad.

Note: Almond mayonnaise recipe can be found in the condiments section of this recipe book.

Mediterranean Salad

Ingredients:

3 - 4 large kale leaves, stalks removed

1/2 cup red bell pepper, diced

1 tablespoon pine nuts

1 tablespoon black olives, sliced

1 1/2 teaspoons extra virgin olive oil

1 1/2 teaspoons lemon juice

Dash of seal salt

Dash black pepper

Directions:

Prep the kale by removing the stems, and chop into bite-size pieces. Place the kale in a mixing bowl, drizzle the lemon and olive oil over the kale. Sprinkle with a little bit of salt, and then use your hands to massage the liquid and salt into the kale leaves. Add the rest of the ingredients and toss together. Let it sit for 30 minutes before serving

Cauliflower "Egg" Salad

Ingredients:

3 cups raw cauliflower

1 cup carrots, shredded

1/2 cup sunflower seeds, soaked

1 cup celery. diced

1/2 cup nutritional yeast

1/2 cup scallions

6 tablespoons mustard

4 tablespoons tahini

1 tablespoon dried parsley

1 tablespoon chia seeds

1 tablespoon dill, dried

2 teaspoons sage, dried

1/2 teaspoon garlic powder

1/2 teaspoon turmeric

1 teaspoon sea salt

1 teaspoon black pepper

1/2 cup water

Directions:

In a small bowl, make the dressing by combining the water, spices, mustard, tahini, chia seeds, relish, salt and pepper. Whisk together well, and chill for at least an hour.

Prep the cauliflower by pulsing it a few times in the food processor, set it aside. Next, add the sunflower seeds and pulse in the food processor, then add the pulsed sunflower seeds to the bowl with the cauliflower. Add the carrots, celery, scallions, and nutritional yeast.

Pour the dressing over the salad mix, and stir well to coat evenly.

Josephine James

Fruit Salad

Ingredients:

1/2 cup blueberries

1 cup grapes

2 pears

2 apples

1/4 cup raspberries

1/3 cup walnuts, chopped

Dressing Ingredients:

2 bananas

1 cup almond milk

2 dates

1/2 a vanilla bean

Directions:

Add dressing ingredients into the blender, and blend well until smooth.

Prepare fruit by washing and chopping the apples and pears. Slice the grapes in half, leave the blueberries as-is. Mix all the fruit together in a large mixing bowl, pour the dressing over the top and stir together to evenly coat.

For a fun twist, add a little bit of chopped, fresh mint to the salad.

Spinach Poppy Seed Salad

Ingredients:

6 cups baby spinach

2 cups strawberries, sliced

2 tablespoons pine nuts or slivered almonds

1/4 cup red onion, thinly sliced

Dressing Ingredients:

1 tablespoon fresh lemon juice

1 tablespoon apple cider vinegar

1 tablespoon olive oil

1 tablespoon maple syrup

1/4 cup raspberries

1 teaspoon poppy seeds

Salt and pepper to taste

Directions:

Add the dressing ingredients into a small mixing bowl, whisk together to incorporate all ingredients together.

Add the spinach, onion, and strawberries in a large mixing bowl, pour the dressing over the top and toss to evenly coat the spinach. Sprinkle the pine nuts on top and serve immediately.

Berry Salad with Vinaigrette Dressing

Salad Ingredients:

Mixed greens of your choice, including spinach, red lettuce, kale, green leaf lettuce, etc.

Fresh raspberries (may be substituted for strawberries, blueberries, or oranges)

Red onion, thinly sliced

Sliced almonds or chopped walnuts

Dressing Ingredients:

1 cup extra virgin olive oil

1/2 cup apple cider vinegar

1 tablespoon honey

1/3 cup raspberries

1 shallot

1/2 tsp sea salt

Directions:

Make the dressing by adding all dressing ingredients except the olive oil into the blender, blend well until a smooth consistency is achieved. During the blending process, slowly drizzle in the olive oil until all of the oil is added.

Assemble your salad as desired. Be creative with berry combinations and different mixtures of leafy greens. Drizzle the salad dressing on the salad, and toss to evenly coat.

Josephine James

Raw Soup Recipes

Soup dishes are commonly thought of as hot, but a raw foodist can enjoy tasty soup without the heating. There are many raw food combinations that can be blended together to create a wonderful blend of tastes, and this section of recipes gives you options if you want a bowl of soup.

To achieve the best consistency with these soup recipes, it is a good idea to use a high powdered blender. Cheap blenders won't achieve the same smoothness that high powered blenders can create. Using a cheap blender may result in a lumpy soup, so it's a good idea to use a high powered blender instead.

Citrus Fruit Soup With Noodles

Ingredients:

1 cup orange juice, freshly squeezed

2 grapefruits, peeled and segmented into bite size pieces

1/4 inch fresh ginger

dill leaves, according to taste (a small handful)

1 cup jicama, spiralized

Directions:

Combine the orange juice, ginger, and dill in the blender. Blend well until it has a smooth consistency. In a serving bowl, add the grapefruit segments as well as the jicama "noodles." Pour the orange juice mixture over the top, and enjoy.

Note: The jicama "noodles" can be substituted for cucumber or zucchini "noodles" instead.

Josephine James

Spanish Gazpacho

Ingredients:

6 cups tomatoes, washed and diced

1 cup onion, chopped

1 cup bush beans, trimmed and chopped

1 red bell pepper, chopped

1 orange bell pepper, chopped

2 cups cucumber, chopped

2 garlic cloves, minced

1 tablespoon extra virgin olive oil

2 teaspoons apple cider vinegar

1/2 teaspoon sea salt

1/4 teaspoon black pepper, freshly ground

Parsley, for decoration

Directions:

Dice the tomatoes. Save the tomato juice, and divide the tomatoes. Set half (3 cups) of the tomatoes aside.

In a blender, add 3 cups of tomatoes, the tomato juice, garlic, black pepper, salt, vinegar, and olive oil. Blend well, until smooth.

Add the rest of the chopped ingredients into a serving bowl, stir gently to mix. Pour the blender mixture over the top, garnish with parsley, and serve.

Vegetable Curry Soup

Ingredients:

2 cups water

1 cup almonds

2 red bell peppers

3 garlic cloves

4 large carrots

2 tablespoons coconut butter

3/4 inch ginger

1/4 cup fresh lime juice

2 lime leaves

1 teaspoon cumin

1 teaspoon turmeric

1 teaspoon curry powder

2 tablespoons kelp powder

1 -2 cups chopped vegetables, such as cabbage, carrots,

zucchini, cauliflower, broccoli, bell peppers, kale, spinach, etc.

Directions:

Put the chopped vegetables in a large bowl. Add all other ingredients in the blender, and blend until it is smooth and creamy.

Pour the blender contents over the chopped vegetables, add additional seasonings if you want a stronger taste.

Spicy Tomato Soup

Ingredients:

1 large tomato, diced

10 sundried tomatoes, chopped

1 large cucumber, juiced

1 very large tomato, juiced

1 lemon, juiced

1 large carrot, juiced

1/2 onion, chopped

1 celery stalk with leaves, chopped

1 red pepper, chopped

1 garlic clove

1 teaspoon ginger powder

1 1/4 teaspoon paprika

2 tablespoons fresh basil

1/4 teaspoon cayenne, to taste

Directions:

Combine everything in the blender and blend well. The spices can be added according to taste, so if you want to "warm" it up try adding more cayenne pepper.

Miso Avocado Soup

Ingredients:

2 avocados, skin and pits removed

3 tablespoons miso

2 tablespoons extra virgin olive oil

2 cups water

1 lime, juiced

1 teaspoon fresh rosemary

1/2 teaspoon chipotle spice

1 small tomato, diced

Parsley sprigs

Directions:

Add all ingredients except the tomato and parsley to the blender, blend well. You may add more water for a thinner soup. Pour into serving bowls and garnish with tomato and parsley.

Tortilla Soup

Ingredients:

2 large tomatoes, chopped

2 red bell peppers, chopped

2 large stalks celery, chopped

2 large carrots, chopped

1 garlic clove

1/4 cup fresh cilantro

1/4 cup sundried tomatoes

3/4 cup water

3 tablespoons extra virgin olive oil

1 tablespoon fresh lime juice

1 teaspoon sea salt

3/4 teaspoon cumin

1/2 teaspoon chili powder

1/4 teaspoon paprika

Dash cayenne pepper

1/3 cup corn

Directions:

Add everything except corn and olive oil in a blender, blend well to achieve a smooth consistency. While blending, slowly add in the olive oil until all the oil has been added.

Pour into serving bowls, garnish with corn. Alternatively, this soup could be served with the raw tortilla chips (recipe in the snacks section of this book).

Creamy Thai Soup

Ingredients:

1 yellow bell pepper

3/4 cup cashews

3 carrots, chopped

2 radishes

2 cups warm water

3/4 cup almond milk

1 tablespoon curry powder

1 tablespoon Nama Shoyu

1 tablespoon agave

1/2 tablespoon jalapeno pepper, chopped

1/2 teaspoon sea salt

1/4 cup green onions, divided

Cilantro sprigs

Directions:

Set aside the cilantro sprigs and 1/8 cup green onions. Add everything else into the blender, and blend until a smooth consistency is achieved.

Pour the soup into serving bowls, and garnish with cilantro and green onions.

Cilantro Celery Soup

Ingredients:

1/2 bunch cilantro

1/2 bunch celery

1/4 cup almond butter

1/4 cup raw tahini

2 garlic cloves

2 tablespoon miso

2 tablespoon fresh lemon juice

1 tablespoon Nama Shoyu

4 cups water

Directions:

Add everything in the blender, and blend until smooth. Start with 2 -3 cups of water, and add more water to achieve desired consistency.

Hearty Chili

Ingredients:

6 tomatoes

1 cup lentil sprouts

1 cup corn

1 carrot, shredded

1 portbella mushroom, chopped

1/2 cup celery, chopped

1 green bell pepper, chopped

1/4 cup Bragg's liquid aminos

1 tablespoon extra virgin olive oil

1 tablespoon agave

1 tablespoon apple cider vinegar

2 teaspoon fresh oregano

2 teaspoons cumin

1 teaspoon chili powder

Pinch of cayenne pepper

Directions:

Sprout the lentils by soaking them for 12 hours, rinse and then sprout for about 2 days.

In a food processor, combine the tomatoes, mushroom, olive oil, Bragg's, oregano, chili powder, cumin, cayenne, vinegar, and agave. Process until a smooth consistency is achieved.

Add the lentils, carrot, celery, bell pepper, and corn to a mixing bowl. Pour the soup base over the veggies, and stir well.

Optional: Warm the chili in the dehydrator at 115 degrees for 2 hours.

Josephine James

Green Pea Soup

Ingredients:

2 cups peas, divided

1 1/2 cups almond milk

1 avocado, skin and pit removed

1 teaspoon salt

1/2 teaspoon freshly ground pepper

1/4 cup onion, minced

Directions:

Divide out 1/2 cup of peas and set aside.

In a blender, add the rest of the peas, avocado, salt, and pepper. Blend well.

Pour the soup into a bowl, add 1/2 cup peas and stir well. Garnish with the minced onion.

Raw Snack Recipes

Snacks keep you going throughout the day, and there are many tasty raw foods snacks that can be enjoyed. Crunchy crackers can be made in the dehydrator, chewy sweet treats can be quickly whipped together, and there are many other recipes that mimic popular cooked snacks.

I like to make a few snacks in advance, so that I have something convenient to reach for whenever I get hungry. They are a delicious way to curb your hunger between meals.

Cheezy Crackers

Ingredients:

1 cup Brazil nuts

1 cup sunflower seeds, soaked for 4 hours

1 cup almonds, soaked for 4 hours

1 red bell pepper, diced

1 large tomato

1/4 cup yellow flax, ground

1/4 cup sundried tomatoes, soaked

1 garlic clove, minced

1 pinch cumin

1 pinch onion powder

1 1/2 teaspoons sea salt

Directions:

Combine all ingredients in a blender or food processor, blend well to create a smooth consistency.
Spread the mixture evenly on dehydrator teflex sheets.
Dry at 105 degrees for 3 hours, then cut into crackers with a pizza cutter. Allow the mixture to continue drying until they are firm enough to flip.

Turn the crackers over onto mesh dehydrator sheets. Continue to dehydrate until they are crispy, usually another 6 - 8 hours.

Josephine James

Raw Onion "Bread"

Ingredients:

1/2 pound onion, sliced

1 cup ground flax seed

1 cup sunflower seeds, soaked for 90 minutes

4 tablespoons poppy seeds

1/4 cup extra virgin olive oil

1/4 cup nama shoyu

Directions:

Add onion, sunflower seeds, olive oil, and nama shoyu to a food processor, and process until smooth. Stir in ground flax and poppy seeds by hand.

Spread evenly on dehydrator teflex sheets, allow to dry at 105 degrees for 5 hours. Flip, and allow them to continue dehydrating for an additional 6 hours. Cut into sliced, and continue dehydrating until crunchy, usually about 18 - 20 hours total.

Deviled "Eggs"

Ingredients:

1 1/2 cups cashews, ground

1/3 cup celery, finely diced

1 green onion, finely diced

2 tablespoons water

Pinch of garlic powder

Pinch of freshly ground black pepper

Paprika, to sprinkle on top

2 cucumbers, sliced in half down the length and hollowed out

Directions:

Add ground cashews, celery, green onion, water, garlic powder, and black pepper to a mixing bowl. Stir well to incorporate all ingredients. Feel free to add a little more water if needed.

Spoon the mixture into the cucumber boats, sprinkle with paprika for color. Chill for 30 minutes before serving.

"Ritzy" Crackers

Ingredients:

2 1/2 cups walnuts, soaked

1/2 cup yellow flax seed, ground

2 1/2 cups shredded zucchini

1/4 cup hemp seed

2 teaspoons sea salt

1/2 cup water

Directions:

Soak the walnuts for at least an hour. Drain the water, and add walnuts to the food processor. Process until a fine consistency is achieved, move the walnuts into a bowl.

Add zucchini to the processor, and process until a similar consistency as the walnuts is achieved. Add zucchini to walnuts. Stir in the flax, hemp, salt, and water. Stir the ingredients well, add more water if needed to make the dough a spreadable consistency.

Spread evenly on teflex dehydrator trays. Dehydrate at 105 degrees for 6 hours, cut into pieces and flip over. Continue drying until crisp.

French Onion Dip

Ingredients:

1 cup water

2 ice cubes

3/4 cup cashews, soaked

1 cup sunflower seeds, soaked

2 tablespoons onion, minced

2 cloves garlic, minced

3 tablespoons nama shoyu

3 tablespoons fresh lemon juice

2 tablespoons apple cider vinegar

1 1.2 teaspoons sea salt

2 dates, pitted

2 green onions

Directions:

Combine all ingredients in the blender, and blend until smooth. May also be made in a food processor.

Best when chilled, and served with veggies or crackers.

Raw Stuffed Mushrooms

Ingredients:

1 package brown button mushrooms

1 cup tomato, chopped

3 garlic cloves, minced

1/3 cup basil leaves, chopped

1/3 cup cilantro leaves, stems removed and chopped

1/3 cup pine nuts

1 tablespoon fresh lemon juice

1 tablespoons Bragg's Liquid Aminos

Directions:

In a food processor, add the garlic, basil, cilantro, pine nuts, lemon juice, and Bragg's. Pulse a few times to chop everything. Add the tomatoes, and pulse 2 or 3 more times to mix everything together. You want to achieve a pesto consistency.

Wash the mushrooms and remove the stems. Stuff the mushrooms with the filling.

Place stuffed mushrooms on dehydrator trays, and dehydrate at 112 degrees for 90 minutes to warm before serving.

Rice Pudding

Ingredients:

1 1/2 cups yellow squash "rice"

1 cup cashews, soaked

3/4 cup water

1 tablespoon agave

1/4 teaspoon sea salt

1 tablespoon vanilla

Optional: Cinnamon or raisins

Directions:

Make the yellow squash "rice" by chopping the squash in the food processor. Pulse it a few times to get the right texture.

Many the cream sauce by adding the cashews, water, agave, salt, and vanilla to the blender. Blend well until smooth.

Pour the cream over the rice, and stir in raisins or cinnamon if desired.

"Cheesy" Kale Chips

Ingredients:

1 kale bunch

1 large red bell pepper, seeds removed

1 cup raw cashews (soaked for a minimum of 2 hours)

4 TBSP lemon juice, freshly squeezed

2 TBSP nutritional yeast

1 TBSP raw agave

1/2 tsp sea salt

1/4 tsp turmeric powder

1/4 tsp onion powder

Directions:

Wash the kale leaves and pat dry with a towel, allow it to dry as much as possible. Tear the leaves into small, bite-size pieces and remove the thick stems.

Make the raw "cheese" sauce by combining all other ingredients in the blender. Blend until smooth.

In a large bowl, combine kale pieces with the sauce. Use your hands to gently coat the kale leaves with the sauce.

Lay the kale leaves on a dehydrator tray, and allow to dehydrate at 118 degrees overnight. The kale chips should stay in the dehydrator a minimum of 6 hours, or until they are dry and crunchy. For best results, use mesh dehydrator trays, or flip the kale chips over halfway through.

Raisin Flax Crackers

Ingredients:

2 cups flax seeds, soaked

2 bananas, peeled

4 cups water

2 cups raisins, divided

1/2 teaspoon sea salt

1/2 teaspoon ground cinnamon

Directions:

Soak the flax seeds for about 2 hours in 4 cups of water, do not strain the water. The flax, water, bananas, 1 1/2 cups raisins, sea salt and cinnamon into a food processor. Run the food processor until the mixture has a smooth consistency. Add in 1/2 cup raisins and stir by hand.

Spread the mixture on teflex dehydrator sheets, dehydrate at 100 degrees for 4 hours. Flip the crackers onto mesh trays, cut them into cracker size. Dehydrate another 6 hours, or until crispy.

Spicy Red Pepper Chips

Ingredients:

6 red bell peppers

2 cups flax, ground

1 cup basil, packed

1 1/2 cups water

1/2 teaspoon cayenne, or more if desired

1 teaspoons chili powder

1 teaspoon sea salt

Directions:

In a food processor, pulse the bell peppers, basil and spices. Add in the flax and water, pulse to combine all ingredients.

Allow the mixture to sit for 30 minutes, then stir well. Spread evenly on teflex dehydrator sheets. Dehydrate for 6 hours at 110 degrees. Cut into squares, and flip onto mesh dehydrator sheets. Dehydrate for 6 hours, or until desired crispiness is achieved.

Cheezy Zucchini Crackers

Ingredients:

2 cups zucchini, cubed

2 cups walnuts, soaked for 30 minutes

1/2 cup flax seed, ground

3/4 c. water

2 tablespoon nutritional yeast

1/2 teaspoon sea salt

Directions:

Combine ground flax and water in a bowl, soak for about an hour. In a food processor, add the zucchini and pulse until the pieces are uniform. Don't over process. Add zucchini to flax meal mixture.

Add walnuts in the food processor, and pulse a few times to chop the walnuts. Combine walnuts with the flax and zucchini.

Stir all ingredients together, spread onto teflex dehydrator sheets and dehydrate at 110 degrees for 8 hours. Cut into crackers and flip, dehydrate another 8 - 10 hours until crispy.

Refried Beans

Ingredients:

2 1/2 cups sunflower seeds, soaked

2 tablespoons raw almond butter

1/4 onion, chopped

2 1/2 teaspoon cumin powder

2 teaspoon chili powder

1 teaspoon sea salt

3/4 cup water

Directions:

Soak the sunflower seeds, 2 1/2 cups of dry seeds will
soak up the water and you will have about 4 cups of
soaked seeds. Drain excess water. Add everything into
the food processor, and blend until smooth. Pour into a
small dish, warm in the dehydrator for 30 minutes at
105 degrees.

Chia Chocolate Crackers

Ingredients:

1 cup chia seeds

2 cups water, divided

1 orange, juiced

1/4 cup raw chocolate powder

1 apple, chopped

6 dates, pitted

2 tablespoons agave

1 pinch sea salt

Directions:

Soak the chia seeds in 1/2 cup water. Combine 1/2 cup water, orange juice, chocolate powder, apple, dates, agave, and sea salt in the blender. Blend well, until a smooth texture is achieved.

Stir blended mixture into the bowl with the chia seeds. Use a spatula to stir well. Allow the mixture to sit for 30 minutes. Spread the mixture on teflex dehydrator sheets, dehydrate at 115 degrees for 60 minutes, then score into crackers and dehydrate at 105 degrees for 8 hours.

Remove crackers from teflex sheets, and flip onto mesh dehydrator trays. Dehydrate for another 8 hours, or until the desired crispiness is achieved.

Banana Bread

Ingredients:

10 dates, pitted

1 cup coconut meat

1/4 cup coconut water

1 banana

1 cup almond pulp

Directions:

Add dates, banana, coconut meat and coconut water in the food processor. Blend well. Add in almond pulp and stir in by hand. Mix well so that ingredients are evenly incorporated.

Form into cookie patties, lay on dehydrator sheets and dehydrate at 115 degrees for 8 hours. Flip them over, and dehydrate another 10 -12 hours, or until desired texture is achieved.

Almond Power Bars

Ingredients:

2 cups almonds, soaked

1/2 cup dried coconut, shredded

1/2 cup almond butter

1/2 cup flax, ground

1/2 cup coconut oil

1/2 teaspon sea salt

2 tablespoon agave

1 tablespoon vanilla

Directions:

In a food processor, add the flax coconut, almonds, salt, and almond butter. Pulse a few times, then add coconut oil, vanilla, and agave. Continue to run the food processor until a thick paste is created. If you have a small food processor, divide the mixture into 2 batches and process each batch individually.
Press the mixture into a glass dish, and chill for 60 minutes in the fridge. Cut into bars, and enjoy. Alternatively, the mixture can be rolled into balls.

Spicy and Sweet Kale Chips

Ingredients:

2 kale bunches

1/4 cup extra virgin olive oil

1/2 lemon, juiced

1 tablespoon agave

1 teaspoon sea salt

cayenne pepper to taste

Directions:

Wash the kale, remove the stems and tear into chip sized pieces. All it to dry as much as possible.

In a mixing bowl, combine the rest of the ingredients and whisk well. Add in the kale pieces, and use your hands to evenly coat the kale. Add more oil if needed.

Dehydrate for 4 hours at 115 degrees. Flip the kale chips, and then dehydrate for another 4 hours or until crispy.

Onion Rings

Ingredients:

1 onion, sliced and separated into rings

1 cup flax, ground

3/4 cup sunflower seeds, ground

4 tablespoons extra virgin olive oil

2 tablespoons water

3 teaspoons paprika

Sea salt and pepper to taste

Directions:

Put the olive oil in a small bowl. In another bowl, combine the flax, sunflower seeds, paprika, sea salt, and pepper. Mix well.

Dip the onion rings into the oil, then into the breading to coat well. Try to get a thick breading on each of the rings.

Dehydrate at 105 degrees for 6 hours. Flip, and dehydrate another 6 hours or until crispy.

Josephine James

Spicy Tortilla Chips

Ingredients:

3 cups fresh corn

1 red bell pepper

2 jalapenos, seeds removed

3/4 cup flax, ground

1/2 cup onion

1 tablespoon lime juice

2 teaspoon sea salt

2 teaspoon cumin

1/2 teaspoon chili powder

Directions:

Add the corn, bell pepper, jalapeno, and onion into a food processor. Process until a smooth consistency is reached. Add the rest of the ingredients, and pulse a few times to combine.

Evenly spread the mixture on teflex dehydrator sheets. Dehydrate for 8 hours at 115 degrees. Remove the chips from the dehydrator sheets and cut into chip sizes. Dehydrate on regular dehydrator trays for another 6 hours, until the desired crispiness is achieved.

Sprouted Chickpea Hummus

Ingredients:

1 cup chickpeas (garbanzo beans), soaked for at least 10 hours

4 cloves of garlic

2 lemons, juiced

1/4 cup extra virgin olive oil

1/4 cup raw tahini

1/8 teaspoon sea salt

1/8 teaspoon cumin

1/4 - 1/2 cup water

Directions:

Add everything in a blender, and blend until smooth.
Start with a small amount of water, and add more as
needed to get the chickpeas to move in the blender.

Great when served with fresh veggies such as
cucumber slices, carrot sticks, or celery sticks. Or,
combine with tortilla chips or crackers.

Josephine James

Raw Condiment Recipes

Condiments are a great way to jazz up a meal and add more flavor, but it is difficult to find raw condiments at the grocery store. These recipes offer some of the common condiments that are often used with cooked meals, but the recipes are much healthier than eating condiments from a jar at the grocery store.

Make the condiments in advance, and store them in the fridge for a few days to enjoy with several different meals.

Ranch Cashew Dip

Ingredients:

1 1/2 cups raw cashews, soaked for 90 minutes and drained

4 teaspoons lemon juice, freshly squeezed

1 teaspoon will weed

1 teaspoon garlic powder

1 teaspoon onion powder

1 teaspoon sea salt

1 teaspoon basil

1 teaspoon Italian seasoning

Directions:

In a blender, add the cashews, lemon juice, garlic powder, onion powder, sea salt, and 1 cup water. Blend until smooth, and pour into a serving bowl.
By hand, stir in the rest of the seasonings. Serve as a dip with vegetables or raw crackers.

Josephine James

Fresh Salsa

Ingredients:

4 medium tomatoes, diced

1 small red onion, diced

2 garlic cloves, minced

2 peppers, diced (jalapeno or Anaheim depending on preferred spice level)

1/2 cup cilantro leaves, chopped

1 tablespoon apple cider vinegar

1 tablespoon fresh lemon juice

1 tablespoon extra virgin olive oil

1 teaspoon coriander, minced

1 teaspoon cumin, minced

Directions:

Combine coriander, cumin, cilantro, garlic, lemon, vinegar, and oil, stir well.

In a food processor, add the tomato, garlic, onion, and the blend of spices and liquid. Pulse 2 or 3 times, depending on desired consistency.

Allow to sit for 15 minutes before serving.

Fresh Guacamole

Ingredients:

4 avocados

1 tablespoon fresh lime juice

1/2 tsp sea salt

1/4 cup fresh salsa

Directions:

Mash the avocados to remove all chunks. Stir in the salsa.

Sprinkle sea salt and lime juice over the top. Cover and chill in the fridge for 20 minutes before serving.

Barbecue Sauce

Ingredients:

3 cups sundried tomatoes, soaked

2 cups fresh tomatoes, chopped

6 dates, pitted and soaked

1 large onion, chopped

3 garlic cloves

1 teaspoon Liquid Smoke flavoring

1/4 cup fresh lemon juice

1/4 cup raw honey

2 tablespoon raw apple cider vinegar

1 tablespoon nama shoyu

1 teaspoon sea salt

1 tablespoon mustard, dry

1 teaspoon cayenne pepper

Josephine James

Directions:

Soak the sundried tomatoes and dates separately, for at least 2 hours. After soaking, save 1/2 cup of the liquid from the sundried tomatoes and drain the rest.

Combine all ingredients into a blender, keep the soaked sundried tomato water to the side if needed. Blend well, as the sundried tomato water a small amount at a time until the sauce has a good consistency.

Raw Pickles

Ingredients:

3 pounds small pickling cucumbers

4 horseradish leaves

1/2 bunch dill

Garlic cloves

9 tablespoons sea salt

6 cups water

Directions:

Prepare the cucumbers by washing them, and cut a small amount off of each end to remove the stem and open the end. Add the cucumbers into a gallon-size glass jar, along with the dill, horseradish, and garlic cloves.

Mix the water and salt well, blend if needed to completely dissolve the salt. Pour the water over the cucumbers. Be sure the cucumbers are completely covered, add more water if needed. Cover the jar with a cloth, and allow to soak for 4 days. After the pickling process is complete, drain the liquid and store in the fridge.

Eggplant "Bacon" Slices

Ingredients:

1 eggplant

1/4 cup extra virgin olive oil

4 tablespoons apple cider vinegar

2 tablespoons agave

1/2 teaspoon paprika

1/2 teaspoon onion powder

1/4 teaspoon cayenne pepper

Directions:

Slice the eggplant to look like bacon strips.

In a different bowl, combine all other ingredients and mix well. Add the eggplant strips to the liquid sauce, be sure the eggplant is completely covered with the liquid. Soak for at least 2 hours.

After marinating for 2 hours, place the eggplant strips on dehydrator sheets. Dehydrate at 106 degrees for 8 hours, then flip the eggplant slices and dry for another 8 hours or until crispy.

Chipotle Mayonnaise

Ingredients:

2 tablespoons olive oil

1 cup pine nuts

1 lemon, juiced

1 clove garlic

1/2 Cup young coconut meat

1/4 Cup water

3 teaspoon chipotle seasoning

Directions:

Add everything into the blender, blend well. The texture should be smooth with an even consistency.

Raw Almond Mayonnaise

Ingredients:

1 cup almonds, soaked

1 lemon, juiced

1/4 cup extra virgin olive oil

1/4 cup water

1/2 teaspoon sea salt

4 dates, soaked for 30 minutes

Directions:

In the blender, add the almonds, lemon juice, water, sea salt and dates. Blend until everything is mixed together.

During the blending process, drizzle in the olive oil slowly until all of the olive oil has been added.

Mustard

Ingredients:

3/4 cup apple cider vinegar

1/4 cup mustard seeds (brown)

1/4 cup yellow mustard seeds

1/4 teaspoon sea salt

1/3 cup water

1 1/2 teaspoons agave

1/4 teaspoon turmeric

Directions:

Soak mustard seeds for 2 days in apple cider vinegar. Be sure they are completely submerged while soaking.

After 2 days of soaking, add mustard seeds with the remaining liquid into the blender. Also add the rest of the ingredients. Blend well until a smooth consistency is achieved.

For honey mustard, add 1/2 cup raw honey.

Ranch Dressing

Ingredients:

1 cup cashews, soaked

1 cup water

1 lemon, juiced

3 tablespoons dried onion flakes

1 1/2 teaspoon sea salt

A dash of black pepper, freshly ground

3 tablespoons fresh dill

Directions:

Soak cashews, and rinse well. Add the cashews, water, lemon juice, onion flakes, sea salt, and black pepper in the blender. Blend well, until smooth. Add more water if needed to achieve the desired consistency. Stir in the dill by hand.

Almond Milk

Ingredients:

1 cup raw almonds, soaked for 12 hours

4 cups water

1/4 cup agave

1 teaspoon vanilla

Directions:

After soaking the almonds well for 12 hours, rinse and drain well.

Add everything into the blender, blend on high speed until the almonds are blended well.

For a smooth texture, pour the almond milk through a cheesecloth. Put the cheesecloth over a large bowl or a jar, and pour the almond milk over the cheesecloth so that it filters through to the container.

If you want thicker milk, then the cheesecloth is not needed, just stir the milk before drinking.

Josephine James

Cucumber Dressing

Ingredients:

1 cucumber, peeled chopped

1 ripe avocado, skin and pit removed

2 green onions

4 fresh basil leaves

3/4 cup cilantro

1/4 cup extra virgin olive oil

1/4 cup flax oil

2 tablespoons apple cider vinegar

2 tablespoons honey

1 teaspoon fresh dill

1 teaspoon sea salt

Directions:

Add everything to a blender, and blend well until a smooth consistency is achieved.

Serve as a dip for raw crackers, a fresh vegetable tray, dressing for a raw burger, or on top of a salad.

Josephine James

Raw Dessert Recipes

No need to feel guilty about eating dessert when all of the ingredients are raw! There are many tasty dessert recipes that can be prepared to please your sweet tooth, and they can be enjoyed anytime during the day since they are filled with high-nutrient ingredients.

The best part about raw desserts is the fact that you don't have to deal with the "sugar crash" that often happens after eating conventional desserts. Raw desserts are full of ingredients that are good for your health, so you can enjoy a treat and support good health at the same time.

Chocolate Crisps

Ingredients:

2 tablespoons raw cacao powder

2 tablespoons cacao butter

2 tablespoons coconut oil

1 teaspoon raw vanilla powder

2 tablespoons maple syrup

2 cups shredded coconut

1 pinch sea salt

Directions:

Put the coconut oil and cacao butter in a small glass bowl, set it in a shallow pan with 1 inch of warm water to melt the coconut oil and cacao butter together. Add in the cacao, agave, vanilla, and salt. Stir well.

In a medium size bowl, pour the chocolate sauce over the coconut and mix well to coat the coconut evenly with the chocolate. Spoon into molds, such as small chocolate tins, or form into mounds. Freeze for 30 minutes to set the chocolate, store in the fridge until serving time.

Raw Coconut Ice Cream

Ingredients:

3 cups coconut, both the coconut water and meat blended together

1/4 cup agave

1 teaspoon vanilla bean

1/4 teaspoon sea salt

Directions:

In a high powered blender, mix all ingredients together until smooth. Freeze the mixture in ice cube trays, keeping 1 cup unfrozen in the fridge.

Once the coconut milk ice cubes are frozen, combine the frozen cubes with the liquid from the fridge and blend together to create a creamy consistency. Eat immediately.

Note: This recipe is a basic ice cream base. Be creative and try adding other flavors, such as fruit or cacao.

Raw Brownies

Ingredients:

10 dates, pitted

1 1/2 cups walnuts

1/2 teaspoon vanilla

1/3 cup cacao

2 teaspoons water

Directions:

Add dates and walnuts in a food processor, and process until well combined. Next, add the rest of the ingredients and process until you have a good consistency.

Press the mixture into a shallow dish or pan, chill in the refrigerator for at least 90 minutes.

Raw "Peanut Butter" Cups

Ingredients:

Almond butter

1/2 cup coconut oil, melted

3 tablespoons cacao powder

A pinch of sea salt

1/4 cup agave

Directions:

In the blender, add the coconut oil, cacao powder, sea salt and agave. Blend well until smooth.

Using a small muffin tin, line the muffin tins with candy papers or candy foils. Spoon the chocolate mixture into each of the muffin tins. Allow the chocolate to harden slightly by placing it in the freezer for 60 seconds.

Next, add a dollup of almond butter into the center of each chocolate. Store in the fridge to harden.

Frosted Sugar Cookies

Cookie Ingredients:

2 cups golden raisins

2 cups chopped walnuts

Frosting Ingredients:

1 cup dates, soaked and pits removed

1 large lemon, juiced

Directions:

Add the walnuts to the food processor, and chop well. Next, add the raisings a little bit at a time, continue processing until well combined. The dough will be thick, use your hands to form cookies.

To make the frosting, drain the dates and combine them with the lemon juice in a food processor. Process until a creamy texture is achieved. Spread the frosting on the cookies and enjoy.

Key Lime Pie

Crust Ingredients:

2 cups dried coconut flakes, divided

1 cup raisins

1 cup dates, pitted

1/2 cup pecans

1 tablespoon pure vanilla

Filling Ingredients:

3 avocados

1/2 cup lime juice

1/2 cup agave

1 tablespoon lime zest

Pinch of sea salt

1 teaspoon coconut oil

Directions:

Make the crust in the food processor, add the pecans and grind to a find texture. Add in the raising and dates, process until the consistency is like a dough. Stir in 1 cup coconut flakes by hand.

In a pie tin, sprinkle 1 cup coconut flakes along the bottom of the pan. Use a spoon to press the pecan mixture into the pan.

Make the filling in a high speed blender. Add all ingredients and blend well. Pour filling over the crust, and allow it to chill in the fridge for at least an hour before serving.

Josephine James

Raspberry Chocolate Cake

Cake Ingredients:

3 cups walnuts

20 dates, pitted

2/3 cup cacao powder

1 teaspoon vanilla

1/4 teaspoon sea salt

Whole raspberries

Sauce Ingredients:

1/2 cup raspberries

1/4 cup agave

1/4 cup water

Directions:

In a food processor, add the walnuts and process until a fine consistency. Add the sea salt, cacao powder, dates, and vanilla. Run the food processor until it forms a sticky dough.

Use your hands to form half of the mixture on a plate, then layer on the raspberries, and finish with the rest of the mixture on top.

Make the raspberry sauce in the blender or food processor. Add all sauce ingredients and blend well, until smooth.

Drizzle the sauce over the chocolate cake, garnish with fresh raspberries if desired.

Chocolate Ice Cream

Ingredients:

1 cup cashews, soaked

1 cup water

1/2 cup agave

3 tablespoons cacao powder

2 teaspoons Vanilla

3 - 4 cups ice cubes

Directions:

Add all ingredients in a high powered blender and blend until smooth. For thicker ice cream, add more ice cubes.

Eat immediately. Or, freeze in ice cube trays, and set aside a little bit of the mixture in the fridge. When you are ready to eat the ice cream, add the frozen ice cubes with the mixture and the mixture from the fridge into the blender, blend well.

Cinnamon Pecan Balls

Ingredients:

1 cup pecans, soaked

1 cup dates, pitted and soaked

1/2 teaspoon cinnamon

1 tablespoon orange zest

pinch of sea salt

Directions:

Soak the pecans for 8 hours, soak the dates for 30 minutes. Drain well.

Add the dates into a food processor, and run the processor until they form into a ball. Spread the date mixture evenly around the bowl, and add in the rest of the ingredients. Scrape the sides as needed, process until smooth.

Form into round balls, store in the fridge until you are ready to eat them.

Strawberry Coconut Macaroons

Ingredients:

3 cup shredded coconut

1/3 cup dates, pitted

1 1/2 cup strawberries

2 tablespoons flax seeds, ground

1/4 cup agave

1 tablespoon coconut oil, melted

Directions:

Add everything to the food processor, process for 10 seconds or until everything is mixed together to form a dough. Use your hands to pinch off a piece of the dough, and roll into a ball. Line a plate with parchment paper, and place the macaroons on the lined plate.

Store in the fridge at least 4 hours before serving. Keep them in the fridge in an airtight container until they are eaten.

Almond and Walnut Fudge

Ingredients:

1 cup almond butter

1/2 cup walnuts, chopped.

1/2 cup cacao powder

1/4 cup agave

Directions:

In a mixing bowl, add the cacoa powder, almond butter and agave. Use your hands to mix everything together. You can use a spoon, but it's usually easiest with your hands since it's a thick consistency.

Once the fudge ingredients are combined well, add in the chopped walnuts and mix in evenly.

Press into an 8x8 pan, store in the fridge for at least 3 hours before serving.

Cherry Almond Pudding

Ingredients:

2 cups cherries, pitted

1/2 cup cashews

1 1/2 tablespoons maple syrup

2 tablespoons coconut butter, melted

1 tablespoon coconut oil, melted

1/2 teaspoon vanilla

Directions:

In a blender, add everything except the coconut oil and coconut butter. Blend well, to get a smooth consistency. Add in the oil and butter, blend again to mix everything together.

Store in the fridge for at least 6 - 8 hours before eating. For garnishment, it can be topped with chopped walnuts or almonds.

Raw Cookie Dough

Ingredients:

2 cups macadamia nuts

2 young coconuts, meat only

1 cup coconut flakes

1 tablespoon coconut oil, melted

2 tablespoons agave

1 teaspoon pure vanilla

Pinch of sea salt

Directions:

In a food processor, add the coconut meat and process until smooth. Then add in the vanilla, salt, and agave and process again. Next, add in the macadamia nuts, pulse a little bit to leave texture in the dough.

Roll dough into small balls, and store them in the fridge for 2 hours before serving.

Chocolate Milk Shake

Ingredients:

4 bananas, peeled and frozen

6 dates, pitted

2 cups almond milk

A dash of sea salt

1 teaspoon vanilla

3 tablespoons cacao powder

Ice, if needed

Directions:

Add everything to a blender and blend well. If you want a thicker shake, add ice until it achieves the desired thickness. Drink immediately.

6900210R00097

Printed in Great Britain
by Amazon.co.uk, Ltd.,
Marston Gate.